For all the children who inspired countless Socemo Books
and to the AWA Square Squad; Dana, Shazia, Mary, Abby,
Millie & Craig.

Special thanks to Millie Williams for text artistry!

Note to the Important Adults:

What is a Socemo Book? It is a story to share again and again with your child that covers social-emotional topics. Think of it as a 'how to do things' story.

This book is best read together- adult & child- so you can share times when you felt the same way or when the same thing happened to you. Sometimes diving into topics like this can bring back feelings and memories of your own childhood.

Be brave and share how you felt and what you did when you were learning about consent. This will deepen the connection between you and your child and remind them that they are not alone.

You got this!
Amy

Consent. What is That Anyway?

A Socemo Book

About Consent

By Amy Williams

What is consent anyway?

Consent means to give someone permission to do something.

Like kisses, snuggles, holding hands, playing rough on the playground, chasing each other, or borrowing something.

Your body belongs to YOU.
Nobody should touch it in ways
that you don't like.

You might like
hugs and kisses.

Or not...

It's the same for

everyone else.

You might like hugs, but that doesn't mean that everyone likes them.

Feel like hugging someone?

Ask them first.

Let's practice.

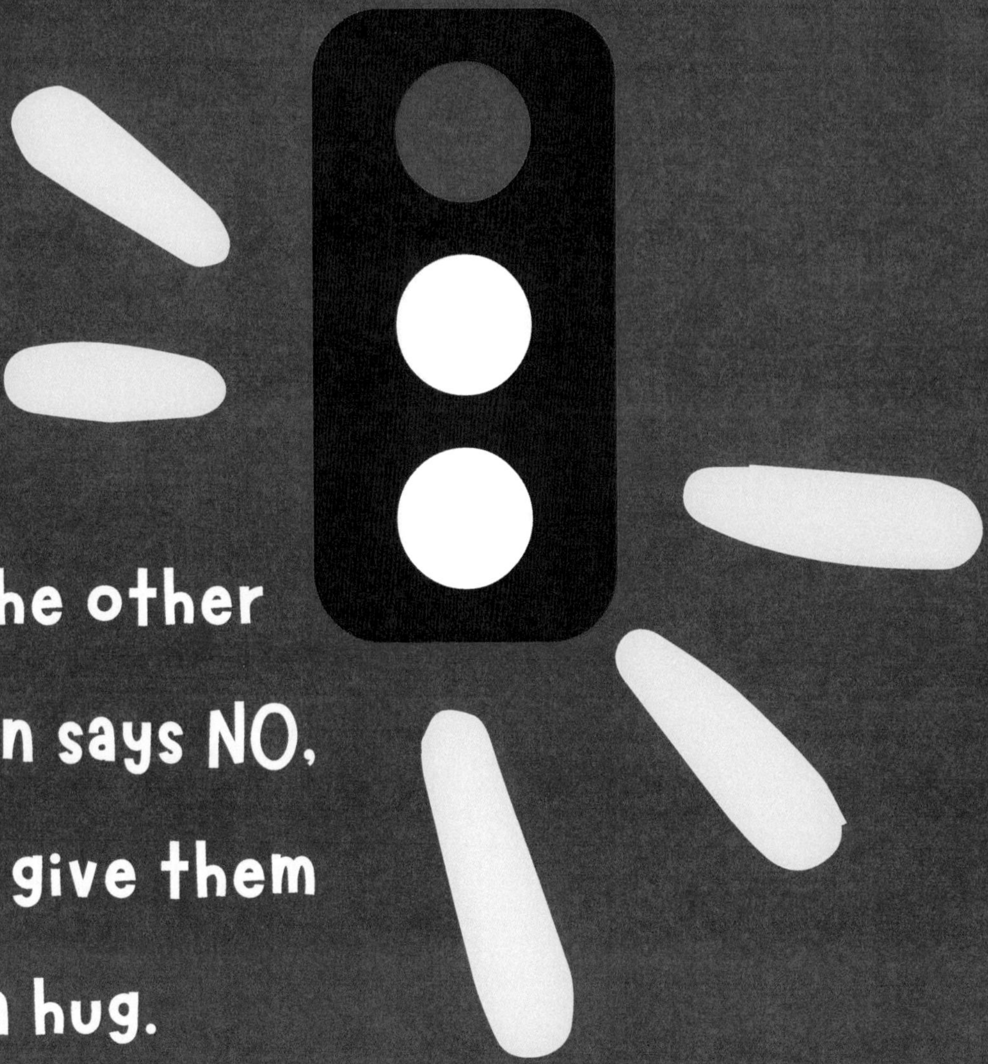

If the other
person says NO,
don't give them
a hug.

Let's practice.

You can wink.

You can bow.

You can wave.

If the other person doesn't say
"YES", don't hug them.

They might think it will hurt your feelings or make you angry.

It doesn't mean they want a hug.

No "YES"
=
No hug.

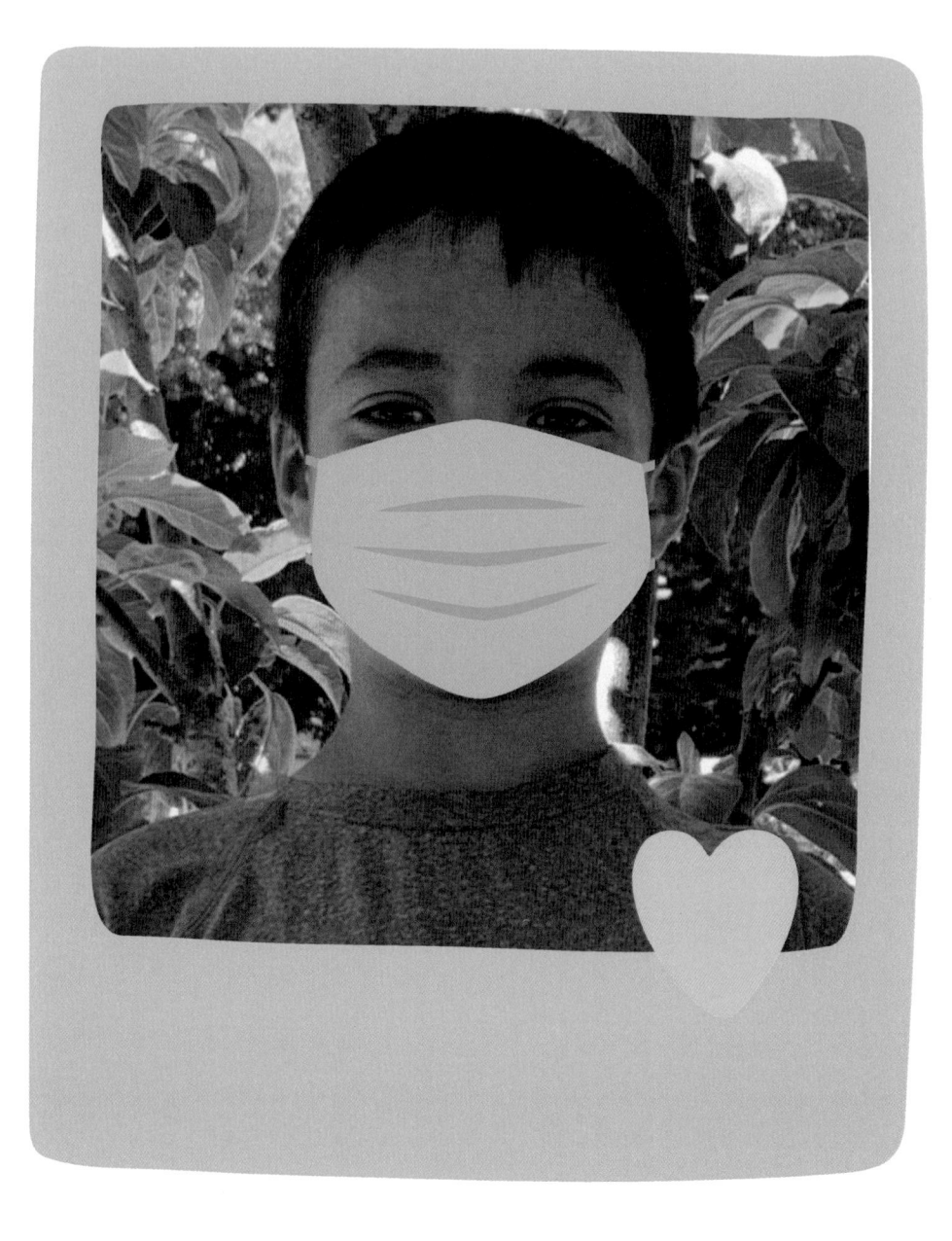

When we wear a mask, it can be hard for others to hear our voices and understand what we are saying.

That can be very

annoying.

You can try to speak

louder.

You may have to repeat
yourself so they can
understand.

You may have to ask others to

repeat

themselves so you can understand them.

Let's practice our

ENTHUSIASTIC

"YES!"

Let's practice our
firm, clear
"NO".

If they wanted to play yesterday,
that doesn't mean that they want to
play today.

Ask every time.

But what if they started a hug or started playing and then changed their mind?

That means stop.

This means that they do not want to keep playing.

You may feel disappointed, but you can try again later.

Maybe tomorrow.

This applies to
grown-ups too.

Adults should not hug or kiss you, play rough, or borrow something without your consent.

Sometimes, an adult may have to touch us when we are in danger or may be sick.

Your favorite grown-up can be with you. They can let you know what is going to happen so you know.

Your body belongs to you and nobody should touch it without your consent.

Other people's bodies belong to them and you shouldn't touch it without their consent.

Let's practice our

ENTHUSIASTIC

"YES!" again.

Let's practice our
firm, clear
"NO." again.

Your body belongs to you.

Nobody should touch it in ways that you don't like.

Notes to all the important adults in the lives of children:

- Have this conversation early and often.
- Role model asking for and respecting consent from the very beginning.
- Remind other adults to respect your child's "yes" or "no." Step in to help if they do not.
- This is important.

You got this!

Share your thoughts!
Tell someone, share a
photo or give this book
as a gift to someone.

@amywilliamsacademy

Made in the USA
Monee, IL
10 November 2024